# EDIE'S
## *Tale*

*With love to my daughter Patricia*
*for her help and encouragement*
*in writing my memoirs*

# EDIE'S
# *Tale*
### *Growing Up in*
### DARLASTON

### EDITH RUSHTON

### FOREWORD BY DR CARL CHINN MBE

SUTTON PUBLISHING

First published in 2005 by
Sutton Publishing Limited · Phoenix Mill
Thrupp · Stroud · Gloucestershire · GL5 2BU

Edith Rushton has asserted the moral right to be identified as the
author of this work.

British Library Cataloguing in Publication Data
A catalogue record for this book is available from the British Library.

ISBN 0-7509-4326-2

Typeset in 12/17pt ACaslon Regular.
Typesetting and origination by
Sutton Publishing Limited.
Printed and bound in England by
J.H. Haynes & Co. Ltd, Sparkford.

# Contents

# Foreword

## By Dr Carl Chinn

They used to reckon that when Rubery Owen's knocked off for dinner time, the throng of workers was so great pouring out of the factory and into Darlaston town centre that people had to walk four deep along the footpath. A small Black Country town with a population of less than 20,000, Darlaston boasted not only the great Rubery Owen's but also the big works of GKN where all kinds of nuts and bolts were made. In fact, so huge was the output from this and other factories that Darlaston was undoubtedly the nuts and bolts capital of the world. It may have been small, but through the importance of its wares, Darlaston punched well above its weight on the world stage.

Lying just over a mile north-west of Wednesbury and 3 miles south-west of Walsall, Darlaston was recorded as Derlaveston in 1262 and as Derlaston by 1316. Noted from the late 1600s for its nails and coal, by the early nineteenth century Darlaston was also marked out by its gun-lock-makers. In 1834 in his *History, Gazetteer and Directory of Staffordshire*, William White explained that 'the manufacture of the place is gunlocks; and there are several steel furnaces and forges for the supply of steel for the locks and springs that are made'.

During the long French Wars from 1791 to 1815, the gun-lock-makers of Darlaston prospered because 'the workmen are incredibly ingenious, being able to forge almost anything on the anvil'. So they could, but the coming of peace in 1815 led to a depression generally in

Britain and to a decline in the fortunes of the Darlaston gun-lock-makers. Despite this the trade remained an important one. By 1861 there were 5 or 6 main workshops in the town, each employing about 20 skilled men; and there were between 20 and 30 little masters. However, because of mechanisation and the emergence of gun production in other countries the end was fast approaching for the trade,

The final blow came in the depression which afflicted gun-making after the end of the Franco-Prussian War in 1876. Within fifteen years the gun-lock tradesmen had disappeared from Darlaston. The sad fate of these Darlaston chaps was that of all skilled workers whose craft was destroyed by mechanisation and it was shared by the nailers of the town whose trade became extinct in the same years. The harsh economic conditions were made worse by the closing of local mines and the collapse in the 1880s of two major employers.

Battered by hard times, Darlaston's population fell from 14,739 in 1871 to 13,900 ten years later. Fortunately new jobs soon arose because of the adaptability of some of the town's gun-lock-makers, such as William Wilkes of Eldon Street. By 1865, he had also moved into the production of nuts and bolts – as had John Archer and Son of Great Croft Street and Pinfold Street. There were another fifteen businesses involved in this trade. They laid the foundation for Darlaston to push itself to the fore as the nuts and bolts capital of the world.

For many years, this industry was characterised by small-scale operations. In 1851 Alexander Cotterill was the largest employer with just fourteen men. A decade later he had expanded to give work to 75, but within a few years such a number had been dwarfed by those employed in large factories. By 1911, between six and seven thousand people were engaged in making nuts and bolts in the Black Country, the great majority of them in Darlaston. Perhaps half of them were employed by Guest Keen and Nettlefold's, which had taken over the Atlas Works at the turn of the twentieth century.

Edith Rushton's evocative and insightful life story brings to life Darlaston during the town's manufacturing heyday in the 1930s. Growing up in Foster Street in the heart of Darlaston and living for much of her childhood behind the shop run by her Mom, Edie was in a prime position to see Darlaston as it was for those who made it – its working class. Her own street was as vital as the Hope Street in Salford written about by Robert Roberts in *The Classic Slum*, or the Church Street called to mind by Arthur Harding in his recollections of life in the Nichol in London's East End. Foster Street boasted five sweet shops, one greengrocer, two pubs, a pawnbroker, an old lady who sold lamp oil, another who sold sand for floor coverings, and her own family's general stores.

The street itself was filled with old red-brick houses, many of which were lined up in terraces in courts, which had communal brew houses, miskins, wells and privies. This shared life forced out privacy but it led to strong neighbourhood loyalties and to an awareness of what was going on all around. Youngsters played all sorts of games in and around the street, from marlies to jack stones, and they were enchanted by characters like Alice the Milk and Billy Muggins who had bostin' bargains for a tanner or a bob.

*Edie's Tale* is a wonderful account not only of her own childhood and teenage years and of her own family, but also of the people of Foster Street and Darlaston. Unlike some industrial regions, the Black Country boasts few autobiographers from the working class. That gap needs to be filled so that both outsiders and local young people will be aware of the skills, determination, doggedness and sheer hard graft of Black Country folk. *Edie's Tale* leads the way.

Professor Carl Chinn
October 2005

# This is Edie's Tale

I was born on 27 July 1918, a few months before the first great world war ended, in the middle of a heatwave, so I was told, weighing about 6lb: not very big, but quite healthy. I had a peculiar habit of sleeping with both arms outstretched above my head, as if I was getting ready for a dive. When I was inspected at a few days old by a procession of the older neighbours, which seemed to be the custom at that time, my mother was duly informed that babies who slept in this fashion never lived to be reared. As I am now 86 years old, I think that this 'old wives' tale' can be discounted.

Old wives' tale discounted. Edie, aged 86, still enjoying life in her back garden in Bloxwich, Walsall. (*Mrs E. Rushton*)

# 1

---

# Daily Life in Darlaston

I was born in Foster Street, in a town called Darlaston, in an area of the Midlands generally known as 'the Black Country', which had grown up largely as a result of the Industrial Revolution. There were factories everywhere. Many began in quite a small way and gradually grew into much larger concerns, as the public were able to afford, and demanded, more and more cars, bikes, washing machines, etc. From these factories came a large amount of waste, which was piled up into 'spoil heaps' in various places, black and uninviting until bits of greenery seeded and – with a struggle – survived. Factory chimneys belched out clouds of black smoke and soot every day, which settled on everything around – plants, people or washing on the line. We accepted it as a part of life because we had grown up with it, and it was only if you went out for an occasional trip into the outer country

The canal arm, Old Birchills, off Wolverhampton Road, Walsall. A 1960s woodcut by Geoffrey Oakley (Edie's son-in-law). (*Mrs Pat Oakley*)

The last steam tram at King's Hill on the Wednesbury–Walsall route, *c.* 15 June 1904.
(*Walsall Local History Society*)

Moxley canal bridge, between Darlaston and Wednesbury, no longer in use.

Flour mills, near the canal arm, Old Birchills, off Wolverhampton Road, Walsall. This was part of the industrial Black Country, but is no longer operational.

This building near the canal arm in Wolverhampton Road, Walsall, was also part of the Black Country industrial heritage. It was known as 'the Mission' and gave assistance to the canal people of Walsall (in a similar way to the Salvation Army). During recent years the building was used as the Canal Museum, but closed in 2003 because of a lack of funding. All illustrations on this page are 1960s woodcuts by Geoffrey Oakley. (*Mrs Pat Oakley*)

area that you realised that England was not the same all over. There were also lots of canals and railway lines to transport the profusion of goods. In fact, I once heard it said that there were more canals around Birmingham and the Black Country than in Venice.

There were many small shops in Darlaston. In Foster Street, we had five sweet shops, one greengrocer, two public houses and one pawnbroker, as well as my gran's shop. Then there was the old lady who sold lamp oil, and another who sold sand, mostly used for floor covering. If you took a bucket, you got two shovelfuls of sand for 1*d*.

The two public houses always seemed to be busy, particularly at weekends, when wages were paid out. Some men spent too much money on beer and betting and there was nothing left to give their wives to feed the family for the following week. When they finally arrived home there would be arguments and fights, which sometimes resulted in the wives

Bull Stake, Walsall Road, *c.* 1910. Hobson's ironmongers can be seen on the left of this picture. Walsall Road, as the name suggests, was the main route to Darlaston's larger neighbour. (*Mr Ian Bott*)

and all the children being thrown out of the house into the back yard, afraid to go back until the 'old man' had finally dropped off to sleep. Then, on Monday morning, the wives would collect up all the 'Sunday best' clothes and make up a parcel to borrow some money from the pawnshop in order to try and feed the family for the week. Some of

5

Victoria Park, Darlaston. In the distance to the left can be seen the police station of 1899, and the Town Hall to the right. Bounded by Victoria Road and Crescent Road, Victoria Park was opened in 1903. *(Mr Ian Bott)*

them would come into my gran's shop and she would hand out as much bread as they wanted and say, 'Take what you want and pay me when you can.' Well, some paid up and some never did!

Most of the old houses were red brick and joined together in long rows, with spines leading off at intervals, called 'courts'. One of these courts was called 'the Bethel Row'. There must have been about twenty small houses in this row, with an open area at the front giving access to the front doors. Inside each house, there was just one large living room with a fireplace. One door led to the two bedrooms above, and the other to a small back kitchen with a sink. The other door from the kitchen led out at the back to one long, communal back yard with washing lines, maiding tubs and a few 'privies', shared by everyone. (There were no flush toilets, and toilet rolls had not been invented, so all the old newspapers were cut up into squares and hung up to use instead.)

Also, there were no dustbins. At the top of the yard there was a place called a 'miskin', which had a wall around it and two openings – one into our yard, where we were lucky to have only three houses, and another opening on the opposite side to a yard in the next street, which served about ten houses. The whole back yard was surrounded by a high brick wall. In this one court there always seemed to be a small army of

Foster Street, Darlaston, looking towards the Green, in the 1960s. Bilston Shot & Grit Co. is on the left. (*Mr Howard Madeley*)

Foster Street where it joins the Green, with Blockall on the right, in the 1960s.
The Scott Arms pub is on the corner. (*Mr Howard Madeley*)

children playing there. Everybody tipped all their rubbish in the miskin, and when it was full it was emptied by the council, which wasn't very often – about once every few weeks. It was not very sweet-smelling, so that was why it was put at the top of the yard and the children warned not to play in there. Every year there was an outbreak of scarlet fever, which always seemed to coincide with Wakes Week, at the beginning of August. If you got scarlet fever, you were whisked away to the Fever Hospital. These hospitals were everywhere, including Darlaston, as lots of people caught the disease. Not many people died, as sufferers were isolated for six weeks.

When I was very young, there was a well in every back yard which served about six houses. Our well was at the top of the entry. To get the water, we dropped a bucket on the end of a rope and pulled it up again with the rope. When I was about 4, the council put in mains water pipes with taps, but we didn't have any taps in the houses – just one in the brewhouse, which served three houses.

I always wondered how so many people squeezed into these little houses. Most families had lots of children and it puzzled me how they all got into bed. I remember my mother telling us about an auntie who had nineteen children and reared the lot. Some of the children were married with their own children and came back to visit new babies who were already aunts and uncles as soon as they were born.

Houses in Foster Street were compulsorily purchased and demolished to make way for new housing (Edie's mother, Winifred, was forced to sell her home and shop, and was most upset that demolition did not then take place for another ten years!). This view was taken in the 1960s. (*Mr Howard Madeley*)

Some of the houses in Foster Street only had dirt floors, which were sprinkled over with sand bought from the old lady in the street, but my grandad tiled our floors with red tiles. Later on, when linoleum was invented, my dad covered the floors with that and we made 'bodged' rugs, which made it warmer. There were no vacuum cleaners in those days, so the rugs were just taken up and given a good shake in the yard every morning. Bodged rugs were made out of strips cut from old coats and one of my jobs was cutting up the material. There was a steel tool, called a 'bodger', rather like a screwdriver, with a wooden handle at one end and a hook on the other to pull the pieces of material through the sacks. Sugar bags came in hundredweight sacks and you could buy the empty sacks for 6*d*. The larger rugs were quite heavy to handle, so my dad made a wooden frame for the sacks to be nailed on to, which made them easier to work with.

There was no gas or electricity in the old houses. All the cooking was done over the fire or in the oven at the side. In front of the fire was a large hole covered by a heavy iron grid, and the ash from the fire was raked over the slots each morning and any bits of half-burnt fuel were used to relight the fire. Once a week, all the ash was shovelled out of the hole and disposed of, ready for the next week. Over the scrubbed kitchen table there was a large, brass oil lamp, which was cleaned and polished each weekend by my dad. But everyone joined in the weekly brass-polishing sessions, cleaning candlesticks, a fender round the fireplace, horse brasses and the Avery scales in the shop with the old Brasso. The only light in the bedrooms was by candles, or nightlights, which were short, fat candles encased in thin cardboard to keep them from tipping over.

# 2

# Clothing

Women wore ankle-length skirts, black or very dark-coloured, with a white blouse, fitted into the waist, buttoned up quite high to the neck at the front, plus a white or black apron, according to the job in hand. Hand-knitted stockings (very itchy) were worn beneath leather boots, which were fastened by a buttonhook (a small tool with a wooden handle and a hook at the other end). It was pushed through the hole on one side of the boot, hooked round the button and pulled back through the hole to tightly secure the boots, which were fashioned to fit quite snugly around leg and ankle, rather like today's skating boots. Both men and women wore all-wool flannel vests, never taken off at bedtime, but covered with a nightgown or nightshirt for men. On top of the vest, women wore a white, cotton bodice, also buttoned all down the front and fitted to the waist. Then came the corsets (commonly called 'stays'), also fitted tightly into the waist. These were made in two halves, with holes all down the back for stay laces to be threaded through in order to tighten up the garment where necessary. The fronts had large hook fastenings and they all had strips of whalebone or coiled spring steel sewn into them to make sure the body was kept erect at all times. Next came the very full, tight-waisted petticoats and voluminous bloomers, usually lace-edged.

Edie's mother, Winifred Whitehouse, in her working apron in the back yard of the
family home at 39 Foster Street, Darlaston. (*Mrs E. Rushton*)

Mom's everyday outfit would be a fairly long, home-made dress, a pinafore and leather boots. During the working week, Dad wore a calico shirt, boiler suit and cloth cap, but on Sundays, and also on Saturdays if he was taking us out to the theatre, shopping in Birmingham, or the annual fair or circus, he wore a suit and trilby hat.

When going to school in the winter, I had to wear a hand-knitted woollen vest, a Liberty bodice, several petticoats and a warm woollen dress, plus a lace-edged white pinafore, which kept my dress clean so I didn't have to change it very often. I also had hand-knitted, knee-length, woollen socks. All this wool made me itch a lot and I did not like that. I wore leather boots, usually black and calf-length, which were fastened up with the buttonhook. As well as the black boots, we wore bloomers which came down to the knee, made from cotton. We wore the same clothes for games as well. (My mother had to wear boned corsets, so I was glad people had stopped wearing them before I grew up. Liberty bodices were phased out, and bras came in instead, when I was about 14.) At bedtime I had to wear a long, flannel nightdress, worn over the vest which had been worn all day; you never took your vest off, as it was still warm. There were no hot-water bottles, so to warm up the bed we used the oven plate, which was the steel shelf out of the oven, wrapped in several sheets of newspaper. The flannelette nightwear was a fire hazard, as open fires and candles were in general use, and this material was subsequently banned for children's nightwear unless it could be fireproofed.

Another big fire hazard at that time was the celluloid dolls, which were quite lifelike, lightweight and very popular with children. They were inexpensive but highly flammable. I was never allowed to have any celluloid dolls, but did have the 'platter' ones, which had movable arms and legs, and eyes counterbalanced with a lump of lead inside the head, so that the eyes closed when the dolls were laid down.

# 3

## Family

### My Mother's Family

I never saw my great granma, Betsy Mouton, but heard of her from my mother and some of the older visitors to our house. It was said that she was rather small, but always to be obeyed, and that she would retire to her bedroom after Christmas and not reappear until Easter. She must have lived with my gran and grandad, John and Annie Meredith, as my mother said her gran used to tap on the bedroom floor with her stick for attention, and she had to run up the stairs to see what she required. There was a small fireplace in the bedroom and a fire was always kept burning to keep her warm; this needed constant attention. When she had any visitors, pots of tea had to be supplied, to drink while they sat and had a chat. One of the things everyone seemed to remember was my great granma sitting up in bed with a white lace cap on her head.

My gran, Annie Slaid, came originally from the Nottingham area and worked as a cook for a doctor in Birmingham. She could read and write quite well, but told me that school was not free for everyone in those days and it used to cost 1$d$ a week to attend. When she married John Meredith (my grandad) in Walsall in 1891, she moved to Darlaston. They were both in their early thirties and rented an old cottage at 39 Foster Street, with two rooms downstairs, two bedrooms upstairs,

Edie's maternal grandmother, Annie Meredith, *c.* 1910.
A Henri Gascon Studio portrait. (*Mrs E. Rushton*)

a small pantry and a cellar. Originally, No. 39 was the only house in the street and had a large garden at the side, surrounded by fields. There was also an outhouse (known as a brewhouse) with a baking oven and a coal-slack boiler for washing. Slack, a residue from coal, tipped into the cellar and mainly coal dust, was shovelled into the fire underneath the boiler. You couldn't use the slack on the fire in the living room because it would have put out the fire, but it was all right under the boiler because there was a good draught. You could use it on a domestic fire only if you mixed it with other household rubbish, damped it down and packed it in a paper sugar bag. When the fire was burning brightly, you put the sugar bag into the back of the fireplace and it burnt very slowly and kept the fire going longer, without using more-expensive coal.

At the back of the house was an old, brick-built workshop with an open hearth, where my grandad used to work making hand-made belts, and there was also a furnace and a set of large bellows about 6ft square, with two wooden handles to pump air into the furnace. My grandad also had a lathe and a workbench in the workshop, where he made nuts and bolts and repaired anything that needed mending. The remains of the old forge and huge bellows were still there, along with the wood-turning lathe which my dad took over and used for making children's toys from odd bits of wood. He also renovated worn wooden rollers from the old mangles that everyone used on washdays. I can still remember the wooden horse on wheels that Dad made for me one Christmas.

By the time my gran and grandad (John and Annie Meredith) moved into the house in Foster Street, two back-to-back houses had been built onto No. 39, and there was a yard enclosed with a brick wall and an entry to get to the backs of the houses. As she was a good cook, my gran decided to open the front room of the house as a shop. Grandad Meredith fitted out the room with a counter, shelves, cupboards and drawers, all made in his workshop. Gran baked bread twice a day in the

Edie's maternal grandparents, John and Annie Meredith (seated), with their children, Winifred and Sydney, probably in about 1900/1905. (*Mr Brian Whitehouse*)

Studio portrait of Edie's mother, Winifred Whitehouse, as a young woman, *c.* 1912.
(*Mrs E. Rushton*)

old baking oven in the brewhouse. She made jam and pickles, too, which stood in 4lb stone jars around the room on the wooden shelves made by my grandad, all supported by turned wooden pillars that I always admired. There was also a chicken run in the back yard and they sold eggs and occasionally poultry when these were surplus to family requirements. My grandad also had an allotment and sold the fresh produce in the shop.

John and Annie Meredith had two children: Winifred, my mother (born in 1892), and Sydney, my uncle (born in 1896). I don't remember my grandad, John Meredith, as he died in 1915, before I was born, but I was told that he was found dead on his allotment, which he loved. My gran, Annie, was a very good-natured woman. People were very poor at that time and, as I mentioned earlier, if anyone came into the shop wanting a loaf, but had no money, she would just give it to them and say, 'Pay me when you can.' I'm sure she must have lost a lot of money that way. Years later, when she passed the shop on to her daughter, Winifred, all the rules changed and one week's 'strap' had to be paid before the following week's could begin, so she was not very popular with some of her customers, who said she wasn't such a good person as her mother.

My mother was a bright student and, by the age of 12, had progressed through all the classes at the local school and passed all the exams. At that time it was a case of either leaving school or staying on and helping to teach. It was decided, by her parents I suppose, that she should leave school and be apprenticed to a dressmaker. She told me that she was taught to make men's trousers for a shilling a pair. It became a very useful trade, however, as she made all her own clothes and, later on, all her children's clothes. She had a Singer sewing machine, worked with a foot treadle.

I was very fond of my gran. There was a very large bookcase in her living room, full of large, interesting books and maps, which I was

Len Mitchell's cycle shop. In 1914 Len Mitchell moved his cycle business from King's Hill to 8 Pinfold Street, which had previously traded as Sid Frost Cycles. Len, pictured at the shop entrance, retired in 1963. (*Mrs Marion Evans*)

allowed to look at and read when I was able. One of my very favourite stories was a true tale about a young girl called Grace Darling, who used to go out with her dad in the lifeboat to rescue people in trouble in the storms at sea. I read that story over and over again and never got tired of it.

When I was a school kid, playing in the back yard, my gran, then in her mid-seventies, came to her back door and asked me if I would go in and cut her toenails, as she was finding it very difficult to do. So

I obliged; it was quite easy for me and only took me a few minutes. She gave me *6d* and it became a regular job. She must have told her friends, because other old ladies began asking me to cut their toenails too. Some gave me a few sweets but I didn't make any charge; in fact, I thought it was quite an honour to be asked. Only now, when I am old myself, can I understand their problem and that simple things get difficult or perhaps impossible to do when you get old.

One day my gran showed me a small leather pouch with a brown leather thong laced through the top. Inside were some golden sovereigns, which she said she had saved up to share between my brother and me. She asked what we would like to buy with this money and, without any hesitation, we both said 'a new bike'. At this, she was quite horrified and said she could not allow us to have a bike in case we got hurt, but she said she would give the money to my dad to keep, and when she died perhaps we could have our bikes. I was 18 when she died. My dad duly sold the sovereigns for *37s 6d* each – about £30 altogether – and we had our new bikes. My brother, Wilf, spent all his £15 on a beautiful, super-lightweight racing bike called a Silver Sunbeam, which made all his pals really envious. I only spent about three-quarters of my £15 and had a three-speed Rudge Whitworth bike. It was so new, when I got it from the shop you could still smell the paint. I was very proud of my bike and cleaned and polished it every week. I used it all the time and covered several thousands of miles, visiting Barr Beacon, Sutton Park, Kinver Edge, Ludlow, the Wyre Forest, Clee Hills, Clent Hills, Trentham Gardens, Bridgnorth, Wenlock Edge, Bewdley and Abberley Valley. It really was a great present and I was still riding the same bike when I was 50 in 1968. I then sold it for £1 and bought my first small car.

## My Father's Family

I never knew my grandparents on my father's side (Joseph and Annie Whitehouse), as they both died before I was born. My dad, Joseph Whitehouse, was born in 1892 and died in 1954, aged 62. His father also died at the age of 62, both from viral pneumonia. Dad had to leave school as early as was allowed, to find a job with the highest pay to help keep his large family, as his father and mother had both died. So he went to work feeding a furnace, which was very hot and hard work.

One of my dad's sisters was a cripple, called Aunt Annie. She had no use at all in either of her legs and spent all her early years just crawling around the floor in the house. My dad was very fond of Annie and used to carry her around on his back until she grew too heavy. She never went to school, which was a shame as she was quite intelligent and would have loved school. She told me that until she was two years old she was quite all right and could run about with the others; then she was ill and lost the use of her legs. She was always told it was caused by sunstroke but I think it must have been early polio. As her mother died when she was born, she was more or less left to be raised by the other children when their father died too. Eventually all the other children got married and moved and she remained with her sister Alice. When Alice got married, Annie stayed on and helped to look after the children when they arrived, sitting on the floor next to the tin bath, washing and bathing them and helping to feed them. She really enjoyed doing this and all the children loved her very much.

Around this time, one of the local councillors got up a petition and Annie was provided with a wheelchair so she could actually go out. It was quite large and heavy and she used to propel it around by turning the large wheels by hand. She was really delighted with it, however, and used to visit all the local parks with several of her sister's children sitting on her lap or in the tray by her feet. If there was an incline, the larger

Edie's father, Joseph Whitehouse (extreme left), camping with friends. Note the formal dress, which would be unthinkable in a similar situation today. (*Mr Brian Whitehouse*)

children all had to get out and help to push. A bit later on, the old heavy chair was exchanged for one which was much lighter and propelled by a chain-driven front wheel that she could control by turning the handles with her hands; it also had brakes like a bike.

In spite of her disability, Annie was always a very happy person and never complained about anything, but she always wished she had been taken to school to learn to read and write. When her sister Alice and husband both died from tuberculosis, she stayed on with the children and, as she got older, they all looked after her in their turn.

23

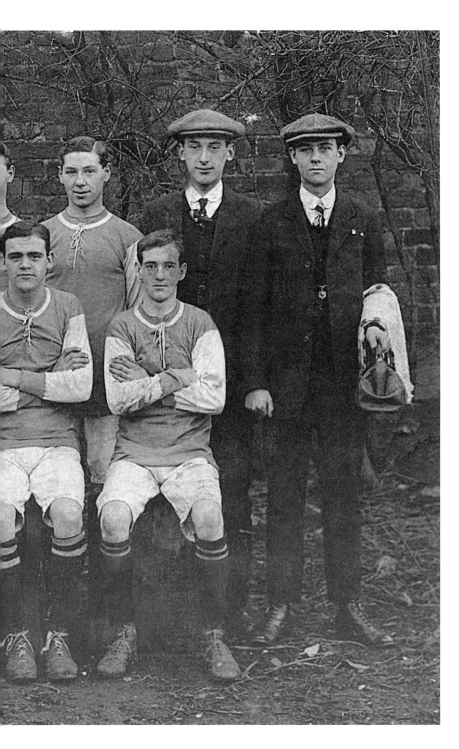

Darlaston amateur football team, with Edie's father, Joseph Whitehouse, third player from the left, back row. (*Mr Brian Whitehouse*)

## *My Brother Wilf*

My brother Wilf always seemed to be getting up to various pranks. One of his favourite tricks was to empty all my jam-jars, containing the fish I had netted in the local pool, down the drain. On another occasion, when Jess the pet dog had three puppies, my mother made her a basin of gruel and my brother tipped it down the sink and filled the dish with coal.

Edie's brother, Wilfred Whitehouse, with dog Scotch on an outing to Blackpool in May 1934. (*Mrs E. Rushton*)

Edie with brother Wilfred on the sands at Rhyl in July 1935. (*Mrs E. Rushton*)

My brother and I were often at odds with each other. He just hated losing. If we played any game, like perhaps ludo, and he was not winning, he would just tip up the board and walk away. Once he smashed the head of my favourite doll with wooden ninepins to get even, so I had to keep a close eye on my dolls, which were all easily breakable.

One day, when I was in the outdoor toilet in the back yard, he got the key and locked me in. He then put the key down the drain and I had to stay there till my dad got home from work and removed the door hinges to get me out. So I guess brother Wilf would call that a win! He was four years younger than me and was mother's darling, so could do no wrong. However, he made a big mistake one day when he popped half a pound of carbolic soap in the teapot just before my dad poured himself a cup of tea. As you can imagine, Dad was not amused.

Edie's brother, Wilfred Whitehouse, with his uncle, Sydney Meredith, *c.* 1930. (*Mrs E. Rushton*)

Edie's brother, Wilfred, on the Menai Suspension Bridge in 1935. (*Mrs E. Rushton*)

# 4

## My Parents' Marriage & Life Together

My parents were married in June 1917 and moved into a small, back-to-back house, next to my grandparents' shop in the same yard in Foster Street. When I was 4 years old, a bouncing baby brother arrived on the scene. This was in 1922. A recession in trade developed and there was a great slump. Lots of people were out of work, including my dad. He spent lots of time tramping around local factories looking for any kind of work, which was virtually non-existent. There was no work and no money. My mother was so worried that she had a nervous breakdown; she was quite ill and went down to about 6st in weight, although she gradually recovered. At this time we were living next door to my gran, Annie Meredith, who still kept the small shop in the front room of her house. Gran decided to give the shop to my mom and dad; they exchanged houses and Mom took over running the shop from my gran. My dad knocked out the small front house window and replaced it with a larger shop window for display. A few years later, the properties (the shop and the two back-to-back houses) came up for sale very cheap – about £130 for all three, I believe – so my gran bought them; but she insisted that they were put in my mother's name, as she didn't want to be bothered with them.

A wedding photo of Edie's parents, Joseph and Winifred Whitehouse, 7 June 1917. Winifred made her own dress. (*Mrs E. Rushton*)

The line of works from Darlaston Green to James Bridge, Darlaston. From the left: Wilkins & Mitchell (Servis); Bradley & Foster (blast furnaces); Martin Winn; Keays; GKN; Owen Recreation Ground (with railings around). In the foreground is the wasteland known as 'the Flats', with coal pickers during the strike. Line drawing by H.R. Arnold. (*Walsall Local History Society*)

While my dad was out of work he was able to get a small amount of money from the Labour Exchange for daily living, but it was all 'on loan' and had to be paid back later. He did finally find a job, thanks to one of his pals who worked in a heavy-engineering company in Darlaston called Wellman, Smith, Owen, and who was able to arrange an interview for my dad. He told him to say 'yes' to everything he was asked if he could do, whether he had ever heard of it or not, and he promised to show my dad anything he wanted to know if he managed to get the job. Well, he got the job, and he never looked back. He worked on all kinds of machines and enjoyed the work very much;

Workers inside Wellman, Smith, Owen in Darlaston. (*Mr John Sutton*)

The exterior of Wellman, Smith, Owen in Darlaston, where Edie's father worked. This is a
modern photograph, but the buildings remain unchanged. (*Mr Stan Griffiths*)

Workers outside
heavy-engineering
company Wellman,
Smith, Owen. Edie's
father, Joseph
Whitehouse, is
second from the left,
middle row.
(*Mr Brian Whitehouse*)

he was quite proud to get his picture taken with a huge crane that he had machined, which was to be sent out to Australia to help build the Sydney Harbour Bridge.

My dad was quite a handyman. He removed the old, black grate in the living room and put in a nice range, which at that time was the sole means of cooking in the oven. Then he knocked a hole in the back wall

Edie's father, Joseph Whitehouse, seated, with dog Jess, outside the back entry of the house in Foster Street.
(*Mrs E. Rushton*)

36

and put in an extra window to make the room lighter. His next job was to build a veranda, joining the house to the outbuilding, making it possible to have a tap inside the veranda, as mains water and gas were now available; so we had a sink and an Ascot water heater, which was a great improvement. Finally, he took the roof off the old workshop, reduced the height by about 2ft and put a new roof on. Needless to say, I was up on the roof with him, helping out! He also got a second-hand enamel, full-size bath and fixed it up in the old bakehouse (brewhouse). There was no hot water on tap, so we had to fill up the wash-boiler and light the fire for that, but this was an advantage as it made the place nice and warm when we were having a bath.

After my dad managed to find a regular job, the old workshop, which he previously used for odd jobs, was used for other things. Firstly, I think, it was for rabbits – to eat, not as pets. However, they did not go on for very long and were replaced by chickens, which were more successful. We all had lots of eggs to eat and to sell, and there was poultry to eat as well. I was quite fond of the chickens, especially when the fluffy yellow chicks were hatched in the nest boxes. There were two feeding sessions each day. My dad gave them wheat each morning before he went off to work, and I usually fed them before bedtime. In the winter all the hens went to roost quite early as soon as it began to get dark, so I had to make sure they were fed before they retired for the night. Otherwise, once they got up on their perches and closed their eyes, they simply refused to move, and if they had had no evening meal, the next day's egg supply dwindled. I found the hens very friendly. There were always lots of feathers around the pen, which I collected so as to spend time floating them from my bedroom window and watching the sparrows diving to catch them to line their nests. All the hens were white and were called White Leghorns and White Wyandots. At this time everyone seemed to prefer white eggs, and the all-white birds always produced all-white eggs.

Just taking a break! Edie's father, Joseph Whitehouse, adopts a casual pose in the yard.
(*Mrs E. Rushton*)

Once there was a large black and white cockerel, called a Plymouth Rock, and it was decided to enter him in the Annual Poultry Show in the Town Hall. To make him look extra smart, a bath was thought to be the order. There were no bathrooms in the old houses, so the old tin bath was brought into the kitchen and filled with warm water and the proud cockerel was duly immersed. But not for long! He strongly objected to the procedure, and as he flapped his way out of the bath there was water and feathers flying all around the kitchen before he was eventually caught.

My favourite parent was quite definitely my dad and I was always allowed to help in whatever he was doing, or I would be quite happy just watching. On the other hand, it was quite obvious that my brother was my mother's favourite. As children, we were always well looked after. I suppose all parents were more strict years ago, and there were rules, which we accepted and obeyed. No swearing was heard or allowed and no lies told. Every night we had to kneel down and say our prayers aloud before we went off to bed. On Sundays, for instance, it would be absolutely taboo to play any games or even sew or knit. Sunday mornings, we went to Sunday School. In the afternoon we went for a long walk and in the evening it was chapel or church, or just singing songs at home.

When I was about 10, my mom thought I should learn to play the piano, as she used to play herself. I must admit that I was not really keen on the idea but after I was assured of a wrist watch if I promised to learn, I said yes. My mother bought a second-hand piano and a music tutor, and every week when the insurance man called, he gave me a music lesson, but if I played a wrong note he gave me a sharp tap with a stick on my fingers. I worked my way through the tutor and got my wrist watch, then promptly gave it up. So my mother played the piano instead and I returned to the allotment with my dad.

My mother used to play the mandolin until my brother accidentally sat on it and broke the stem. Dad tried to mend it but it never sounded quite right, so it was given to us to play with, along with an old fiddle that my grandad used to play and which he had made himself in his workshop.

## The Shop

When my mother took over the shop, she didn't make any jam or bake any bread. She still sold bread but it was delivered by the local baker, fresh and warm each morning, with his horse and van. Before my

No nonsense! Edie's mother, Winifred Whitehouse, stands in the yard with hands on hips. (*Mrs E. Rushton*)

40

brother was old enough to go to the local school, he would wait on the step each morning for the baker to come and then hop up front for a ride with him to the end of the street. He really enjoyed that. Other groceries were bought from the local wholesaler.

We also kept chickens in the back yard and the surplus fresh eggs were sold in the shop. When the fowl had laid a clutch of eggs they went broody, but only one bird was allowed to sit on the eggs, because we needed more eggs and not too many chickens. So if one particular fowl insisted on going broody too often, it was killed off for food. It was my job to keep an eye on the hens to see if any one was going broody too often, as this meant they were not laying any more eggs. Dad would then catch the offender, sharpen up the carving knife and cut its throat, while holding it between his legs over a bowl to catch the blood. I always found this most entertaining; I don't know why but I always liked to watch the operation.

Sugar was not delivered in 2lb bags but in 1cwt sacks, and then it was weighed out into plain, blue 1lb and 2lb bags to sell. When the sacks were empty, they were washed and sold for 6d to make 'bodged' rugs. Salt also came to the shop in large 2ft-square slabs, which dad would cut up with his saw into blocks about the size of house bricks to sell in the shop.

Vinegar arrived in 5-gallon wooden barrels, which would be tapped; a tap would be inserted in the hole and people would bring along cups or small jugs for 'a penn'orth o' vinegar'. Sometimes the children would come for the vinegar and drink half of it before they got back home and then we would get complaints of giving short measure.

Jam was stored in large, stone jars holding about 5lb. It was also sold out loose into a basin or cup, which had to be weighed on the scales first before the jam was scooped out with a large wooden spoon. The lot was then reweighed.

Bacon came in large sides (half a pig), which used to hang in the cellar and were then sliced up when people came to buy it. Some people

Foster Street, Darlaston, looking towards Slater Street, in the 1960s. Opposite the Castle pub on the left is Edie's mother's shop on the right of the picture, with an advertisement outside for 'Players Please'. (*Mr Howard Madeley*)

only bought one slice at a time. On one occasion, after buying one slice of bacon, the customer returned with a little bit of fat out of the middle, saying, 'Can you change this please 'cause my 'usband do'w like fat?'!

Mom didn't sell sweets, chocolates or cigarettes when she first took over the shop, but she did sell Nestlé's full-cream, sweetened, condensed milk, which cost *2d* per tin and contained the equivalent of one and three-quarter pints of full-cream milk, sweetened with sugar. People bought this and used it, instead of buying sugar and fresh milk, for making puddings and putting in tea; it came cheaper and, as there were no household fridges in those days, it kept longer than fresh milk, which soon turned sour in the hot weather. We never actually used this condensed milk at home but always had fresh milk, so I had never tasted it until one day I was visiting a friend a couple of doors away. When I tried it, I thought it was really scrumptious. So, one day when all the family were out somewhere, I got a tin-opener and took a tin of condensed milk out of the shop, and me and the cat ate the lot. Unfortunately, later on, when the family returned home, the cat was sick and I got into trouble for eating the milk. However, I still think it is scrumptious and can eat a canful any day.

I have to admit that I also tried out cigarettes later on when they were being sold in the shop, as I was curious to find out why people came to buy them every single day. Coffin-nails, they called them, and I thought this was because they all had a bad cough. They cost 2d for a packet of five Woodbines. So one day I smuggled a packet into the old workshop and tried just one; but I decided they were quite horrid, so I threw the rest of the packet in the dustbin. I still think they are just as horrid, probably even more so; I just cannot stand that awful smell. It makes people really stink – their hands, clothes, hair – everything smells. If a smoky person sits next to me on the bus, I just have to move away. However, if I'm ever offered a cigarette, I always accept; but when I'm offered a light, it is always, 'No, thank you' – I just put it on my compost heap, where it helps to kill off all the pests.

## The Allotments

Dad took over the allotment at the bottom of Foster Street from my grandad, and we had it for about twenty years. He rented it for 1s a year and grew lots of lovely vegetables and flowers, some of which were also sold in the shop. Previously, my dad had never done any gardening in his life, but his father-in-law, John Meredith, already had the allotment and showed him how to work it, and Dad finally took it over after he died. Some of my happiest times were spent with my dad there.

One of my tasks was spraying the runner beans with water, using a large brass syringe. There were no taps on the site, so water had to be obtained from one of two wells at each end of the allotments, by means of a bucket on a rope dropped into the well and pulled out full of water. I always liked visiting the well, although of course I was not allowed to use the bucket; it was dangerous, as the well was very deep. The well was covered with a wooden top which slid off, but the reason I liked to visit it was because there were lots of big, fat toads underneath the wooden top. When the top was removed, they just sat and looked at you with big eyes, but if you tried to pick one up they would squirt a nasty, horrible-smelling liquid all over you. Frogs were not like this; they looked similar, a bit smaller, but quite friendly. There was a large fresh-water pool by the side of the allotment, full of frogspawn.

One year the beans were covered with blackfly. Someone suggested that smoke would clear them off, so Dad lit a fire in front of the beans; but this was not a great success as it just scorched the plants and had no effect on the blackflies. We had to resort to our original plan of spraying with soft soap, so this was another one of my jobs, which I liked.

At that time we had a little Pomeranian dog called Jess, who also enjoyed coming down to the allotments. She was very good – never walked across the planted parts but always went round on the path. On holidays we didn't go away for a week, but spent most of the time down on the allotment, where we took a picnic and sat on a very small patch of grass at one end. Sometimes my mum came as well, if the shop was shut or it was on a Sunday. We grew lots of lovely vegetables (some of which we sold in Mom's shop), including celery, radishes, peas, beans, beetroot, potatoes, carrots, cauliflowers,

Family pet Jess the Pomeranian dog, outside the entry at the back of 39 Foster Street. (*Mrs E. Rushton*)

parsnips, cabbages, leeks and lettuces. We did not grow tomatoes as we didn't have a greenhouse. There were about twenty allotments altogether and the rent was 1*s* per year. The blackcurrants we tried to grow never did very well, so Dad dug them up and threw them into a pool which was next to the allotment. Lo and behold, the next year they were covered in blackcurrants as big as grapes, so blackcurrants obviously like lots of water!

I had a friend on the allotment called Ben; his dad's allotment was next to ours. I found out later that his name was actually Abendigo and he had two brothers who I did not know, called Ashak and Mashak (out of the Bible). We used to play marbles and other simple games – catching frogs, etc. He was about the same age as me and liked helping his dad on the allotment. He lived at the top of Addenbrooke Street but I never saw him again after the allotments closed down.

In the early years we did not have any problems on our allotment, but later on, a new council house estate was built on the opposite side of the road and then things weren't so good. Although the gardeners were upset when the council estate was built, and the children not only stole the vegetables but broke the plants and destroyed everything, there was nothing we could do about it. Originally the allotment site was down in a dip, and then for some reason it was decided to fill it all in and bring it up to the level of the road, presumably for building on later, but this really spoiled the allotments because the site was filled in with all kinds of rubbish. Nothing ever grew well after that, so people just gave up renting the allotments and it was used for building more houses.

The council decided that the old houses in Darlaston were unfit for human habitation, so put a compulsory purchase order on them and moved the families into the council houses, even though people were quite happy in the old houses. One reason they were happier in the old houses was that the rent for the new council houses was twice as much. Several families lived in one old house with no bathroom or hot and cold water, but the families were split up when they moved into the new houses, which had bathrooms and running water.

# 5

## Local Darlaston Characters

### *Alice the Milk*

In the 1920s, before sterilisation and pasteurisation, milk was delivered to all the houses in our street by 'Alice the Milk'. Her mother and father kept half a dozen cows in a field off Bell Street, Darlaston. After they'd milked the cows, the milk was emptied into churns and loaded onto an old open cart. Alice would harness their old horse to the wooden cart and deliver the milk to local houses. We used to take our jug out to the cart and Alice would turn the tap on the churn and fill the jug. It cost us about *2d* for a jug of milk. We only usually had one pint jug every day for the whole family. Most people drank water or beer from the local pub, of which there were two or three in every street. You took your jug to the pub if you wanted to take your beer home.

One day, one of Alice's customers asked her if she would lend him the horse and cart to remove some items of furniture to another house only a few streets away, but Alice said no, it wasn't possible, because the old horse knew the milk round very well and refused to go anywhere else. So when he got to the top of the street on the way back, having sold all the milk, he just galloped down the street and was put in his field, as his work was finished.

When they started bottling the milk, you couldn't sell raw milk direct from the cow as that had not been sterilised. This was to stamp out TB, which could be contracted from infected cattle. Lots of people had TB – it was rife in those days. People were sent away to sanatoriums to stop it spreading and many died. The cure was to be admitted to a sanatorium because fresh air was supposed to be beneficial, so all windows were left wide open to the elements and there was no heating, even in the winter. People sent to sanatoriums just disappeared; nobody seemed to come home cured. When Alice the Milk's trade disappeared, following the introduction of bottling, she married Arthur Morton, the local baker, because his wife had died when she was only 30. At that time he was delivering bread daily to all the local houses and met Alice the Milk. The local baker's business also folded up when the council condemned his premises because they said it wasn't hygienic, although he had been using it for years and years. He couldn't afford the alterations that the council said needed to be done, so Arthur and Alice, the baker and the milklady, retired and lived happily on the proceeds of the compensation paid them by the council for the premises right in the town centre, which the council used for redevelopment.

## *Billy Muggins and his Bostin' Bargains for a Tanner or a Bob*

Billy Muggins was a local character who lived in Darlaston and must have been about 30 when I was 10 years old. He collected unwanted or damaged items and then sold them off in different streets. These were collected in a heavy hand-made handcart which looked like a large, mobile wooden compost bin. It had two wooden handles at one end and two large, iron wheels. Billy pushed this cart around every day. You could get anything from a picture or an ornament to a brass fender or a fireguard, a pushchair or a bike.

Billy was regarded as 'simple' but he made enough money to live on, as people gathered around his cart, sorting out anything useful or repairable. He was always happy and contented with his lot. Some small items he would sell for 1*d* or 2*d* and say, 'That wo' 'urt ya, wull it, missus?'

# 6

## Some Early Memories

My first recollection is a visit to a photographic studio, Astons on Darlaston Bull Stake, to have my picture taken at the age of 2. It was not common in 1920 for people to have their own cameras. I was all dressed up in Sunday best in a white dress and white pinafore with a frill all round, and white cotton knickers edged with lace, all home-made by my mother. As we walked to the photographic studio a few streets away, I can quite clearly remember having to make frequent stops to hoist up my knickers. Elastic was not in general use at that time and all undergarments were made from white cotton which had a good boiling every Monday morning, so all fastenings were either white linen buttons or white tapes, and thus the final result was 2in of frilly white knickers showing beneath my dress. The photograph was enlarged and framed and duly hung on the wall for all to see. This always raised a smile from visitors; as I got older, I got rather embarrassed and the picture was finally removed to my parents' bedroom wall.

Every morning when I get up, I give my barometer in the hall a tap as I pass by, which gives me a good indication of impending weather and this always reminds me of an incident that happened many years ago, when I was about 9 years old. The district nurse called to give me and my younger brother injections. I can't remember what the

Edie Whitehouse, aged 2. An Aston Studio portrait. (*Mrs E. Rushton*)

injections were for, but one day the nurse dropped her thermometer as she got it out of its wooden container. The glass container was broken, so she tipped the remaining contents of the glass sphere into the wooden container and said I could have it to play with. She said it was called quicksilver and showed me what would happen if I tipped the silver liquid onto a saucer and touched it with my finger. The liquid turned into lots of little silver balls which would all join up together again when we gently shook the saucer. I thought this was quite fascinating and played with it quite often, until one day it fell off the saucer and I lost it because, when it hit the ground, it scattered into many tiny – and unrecoverable – silver droplets. It was not until about seventy years later that I discovered that this silver liquid was actually pure mercury. It doesn't seem to have done me any harm, fortunately, although by all accounts it is known to be very dangerous and a deadly poison.

## My First Visit to Blackpool Illuminations

This tale dates back to 1924 when the Illuminations first began, as Blackpool had just decided on extending its season by putting up lights along the promenade. I was 6 years old at that time and Bertie Johnson, my Uncle Syd's friend, suggested that it would be a nice idea to take a trip to Blackpool to see the much-publicised Illuminations. So plans were made for my mom, dad, baby brother, who was 2 years old, and me to visit Blackpool with Bertie. My mother's friend, Alice Gough, was also invited. Now Mr and Mrs Gough had not had a holiday for several years, as on their last holiday, when they went to Rhyl for a week, their first little girl had caught pneumonia and died before they got home, so they vowed never to go on holiday again. However, then they had a second baby girl, named Dorothy, and, when she was 2 and they were invited to take a trip to Blackpool, they decided to go.

One fine Saturday morning at the beginning of October, Bertie borrowed his father's large car, which was used on weekdays to collect fresh fish from Birmingham market to fry up and sell in the family fish and chip shop. We all piled in the car and set off. I sat on my dad's lap on the front seat, not being a very good traveller, which wasn't helped by the very strong smell of fish pervading the whole car.

All went well until we reached Chester. We were proceeding down a long hill with a line of cars coming up the other side of the road when, quite suddenly and without any warning, a large car pulled out of the line to overtake and bashed head-on into our car. It didn't seem much of a bump; there was not a lot of speed involved and no injuries except a lump on the front of my head when I flew off Dad's lap and bumped into the windscreen. Quite a lot of time was spent in the police station for statements to be taken, and the other driver went on his way, but unfortunately our car was completely out of action and was left in a garage in Preston for repairs, to be collected later. So we took our luggage and all trooped off to the local railway station, where we waited for a train to take us on to Blackpool.

A few miles outside Blackpool, the train came to a halt and we were advised there would be an hour's delay as there were so many trains waiting to use Blackpool station, which was a dead end and had to clear one train out before the next one could enter. Most people got off the train and decided to get on a local tram for the last few miles. Of course, this meant that there was quite a large queue for the tram, with everyone trying to squeeze on. Mrs Gough, with baby Dorothy, was just getting on the tram when it started suddenly and she was thrown on the floor in the roadway. The tram was stopped to investigate the matter. Fortunately she was not badly hurt – a few bruises and torn stockings – and Dorothy and the baby were not hurt, so we were all squeezed back onto the tram and continued our journey into Blackpool. We then got onto another tram to view the Illuminations.

The tram was packed and we had to stand up along the central gangway, so couldn't see anything at all. So, when we came to a stop and noticed a horse-drawn landau standing at the side of the road waiting for passengers for a trip along the prom to view the lights, we all trooped off the tram and got into the landau. I was still awake but the two babies were asleep, as it was about 10.00 p.m. I have never forgotten my one and only ride in a landau. We had a lovely blanket to cover our legs and it was so comfortable, and it was open on all sides, so we had a perfect view of all the lights. We had a nice leisurely ride along the prom down to the South Shore, then turned around, went back to the North End and then back to the centre, where we were dropped off outside the accommodation we had booked for the night.

By now it was just after midnight and all the lights had been turned off. We were all feeling rather tired and looking forward to a night's sleep and perhaps a warm drink. However, when we rang the bell at the digs we had a shock, as the landlady said that we were so late that she thought we weren't coming and she had let our rooms to someone else. There was nowhere else to go as the whole of Blackpool seemed to be packed solid, so we went inside to see what could be done. The three men were found one single bed between them up in the attic, and the landlady agreed to give up her bed for the remainder of the party. We ended up with the two ladies plus three children in one double bed with a row of chairs down one side, covered with cushions. Not the best night ever spent, by any means, and everyone was rather bleary-eyed the next morning.

Next morning there was a bit of a panic in our bedroom when Mrs Gough couldn't find her engagement ring, which she had placed on the shelf behind the bed the night before. However, it must have got knocked off in the general mêlée during the night and, after a thorough search, it was found and was back in its place on the usual finger. So we all got dressed and trooped down to breakfast, only to be told that there was no bread; there were so many visitors in Blackpool that they had run out of it. Anyway, Bert Johnson put on his coat and went out in search of some. After waiting in a long queue, he was finally allowed one loaf, which he brought back for our breakfast.

After breakfast we all trooped back to the railway station and boarded a train for the trip back home, where we were joined in the carriage by another couple with a 2-year-old baby. Before we had travelled far, a large bottle of port-wine appeared from their luggage and they took turns in having a swig out of the bottle, including the youngster. By the time the bottle was empty, they were all a bit woozy and the baby kept repeating, 'I want some more sport.'

James Bridge railway station, Darlaston. The station was opened in 1837 as a halt on the Grand Junction Railway, connecting Birmingham with Warrington. Here, a steam train pulls in, *c.* 1906. (*Mr Ian Bott*)

The journey back home was going well, when Dorothy Gough turned to her mom and said, 'Do you think we might have a train crash on the way back, Mom?' However, we all arrived safely back at Darlaston station, and so ends the saga of our very first trip to Blackpool Illuminations, with my happiest memory being the trip in the landau and the beautiful, shiny-black horse trotting along quite majestically in front of us. Since then it has always been my wish to have another ride along Blackpool prom in a landau.

## Pets

We always had pets around the house, mostly a succession of cats and dogs. They always seemed quite friendly towards each other, but one day we went out for a short while and left our pet Pomeranian Jess and a cat with three kittens in the house. When we came home the dog had killed all the kittens. Jess had several litters, which we sold except for one puppy, named Rex, which was given to my Uncle Sydney. Rex did not like his new home and kept returning to his mom, so in the end we had to keep him. Uncle Sydney taught Rex to sit up and beg.

My favourite pussy-cat, called Sylvia, was mostly black, with a white vest, and was very clever. She came along to watch the dogs begging, thought she was on to a good thing and got in line with them. She sat up on hind legs and waved her front paws in the air, just like the dogs, and when they did a little yap, she did a little mew. Before long, some of her kittens had caught on and soon I had a line of them to supply with titbits. It was quite funny.

I treated all the various animals as playmates. I used to dress up the cats and dogs in doll's clothes, lie them in the doll's pram and take them for walks. The little black Pom bitch didn't mind me dressing her up, but to everyone else she was really snappy. If anyone else even tried to stroke her, she would snap and snarl and never allow them to touch her.

Edie's Uncle Sydney
with Jess in the pram
at the back of the
house in Foster
Street, *c.* 1933.
(*Mrs E. Rushton*)

Family cats begging in the back yard of the house in Foster Street. (*Mrs E. Rushton*)

My tame mice arrived a bit later on, quite by accident, when I attended a Band of Hope meeting at the Methodist Chapel. One of the lads produced a tame black and white mouse from his pocket. He said I could buy it for 1*d*, so I came back home with my new pet and my dad made me a nice mouse cage from an empty soap box from the shop. Then I acquired another mouse, and the mouse family expanded very quickly; there were four litters a year and each litter had from five to nine babies. My dad was kept busy making more and more cages, although I sold a lot of the baby mice to my friends at school for 1*d* each. I thought the mice were quite interesting pets. They were all very tame and I spent hours playing with them and shredding up old twill sheets, which they quickly transformed with their teeth and front paws into nice, round nests, which looked just like tennis balls. Inside these cotton igloos the baby mice would be born, blind and naked, but warm and cosy in the nest. The pet cats were very confused and could never understand why they were encouraged to catch and eat the wild mice, but not allowed to pounce on the tame ones. Finally my mom decided that the tame mice would have to go and I was ordered to get rid of all 200, so I sold them to a laboratory, where they promised to look after them. My dad said I could have some budgerigars instead, so I used the money from selling my mice to buy some blue and green budgerigars. They were quite nice but they were never as interesting as the mice.

My dad made an aviary that had an indoor flight with nest-boxes and an outside one surrounded by double wire netting with a 2in gap in between; this was because the cats would get their paws through single netting and pull out the birds' long tails. Then some of the birds got sick and we found that they were biting the galvanised wire netting and getting poisoned. When we found the first bird obviously not well, we took him out of the aviary and isolated him in a small cage, but he died the next day. Later that same day, an identical bird flew in through the bedroom window and I caught him, threw away the dead bird and put the other one in the cage. When my dad came home from work, he thought a miracle had happened and said, 'You know that bird that looked dead? Well, he's come back to life again.' Sadly, not for very long, as the very next day the new bird died too.

So, we went looking for some new stock and bought a beautiful royal-blue cock bird – not too expensive, so we thought this was a bargain. However – surprise, surprise – he turned out to be 'gay' and only chatted up the other cock birds and completely ignored all the hens. So we took him back and exchanged him, as we were looking for some occupants in the nest-boxes, and eventually we did get a few baby birds.

I also kept caterpillars in matchboxes, with a few green leaves for food. I was not keen on flies, but liked spiders and spent some time catching flies in my hand. I then fed them to the spiders, who would run down from their nest and take them from my fingers. The spiders would feel the vibrations on their web from the flies' feet because I always held them by their wings, so their feet were free to send the message to the spiders. I discovered that the spiders preferred medium-sized flies but did not like big bluebottles because they tended to damage their webs struggling to escape, so I became quite good at catching correct-sized flies with my hands to offer in perfect condition to the waiting spiders.

The Bandstand, Victoria Park, Darlaston, 1931. Darlaston once possessed three bandstands, the others being in George Rose Park and King's Hill. Victoria Park was opened in 1903 and bounded by Victoria Road and Crescent Road. Edie played here as a child. (*Mr Ian Bott*)

## *Games and Pastimes*

It was quite a poor area where we lived and there were lots of other children to play with. Games were quite often associated with the season of the year. One of the first, in early spring, required an iron or wooden hoop and a strong stick for bowling it along in races. Then came top and whip, with tops made of wood, purchased for 1*d* and decorated on the

Boys fishing along the canal near Darlaston Green blast furnaces. They were closed and later dismantled after the 1926 strike. The cupolas have been started up (on the right). Line drawing by H.R. Arnold.
(*Walsall Local History Society*)

A side view (further along canal) of Darlaston blast furnaces, with two boats on canal.
Line drawing by H.R. Arnold. (*Walsall Local History Society*)

top with coloured chalk. The whip was just a stick with a length of string attached to one end to keep the top spinning. Skipping, hopscotch and cricket (with a home-made bat and any old ball) were also popular pastimes, as well as kite flying. Kites could be bought quite cheaply but mainly we spent hours making our own with a few sheets of tissue paper, some string and newspapers, etc. for tails.

Come summer, fishing was very popular, with a penny fishing net and a jam-jar with a handle made from string. There were freshwater pools in the nearby fields, containing leeches, water beetles, tadpoles, etc., but we were mainly interested in the small fish known locally as 'jackbannocks'. I always wondered how all the fish, leeches, water-boatmen and snails got into the ponds, which were surrounded by roads and railway lines on all sides, and I must admit I have never found out. The tadpoles I could understand, as the frogs were able to move around across the fields. Occasionally we migrated a bit further afield to the local canals. One of my favourite places was Simmonds' Pond, down 'the Flats' in Darlaston, just a few minutes' walk from our house. One day my friend and I came home with a jar of tadpoles instead of fish, and my friend left hers in the bottom of the maiding tub. Her mother was not pleased a few days later to find the tub full of baby frogs jumping everywhere. Most of these places have now disappeared and houses or blocks of flats are there instead.

We played at schools, of course, with more of the old soapboxes from the shop being used as seats and desks in the back yard. There were lots of these empty boxes to use, as the soap in those times was not wrapped in separate packages and delivered in cardboard cartons, but came in half-pound blocks nailed up in wooden boxes. We also played shops, and doctors and nurses.

Another of our favourite pastimes was dressing up in some of the old clothes still stowed away in drawers and boxes. The waist sizes were so tight that we were hardly able to fasten the buttons, although they had

Soapbox school. Edie and some friends play in the yard of No. 39.
(*Mrs E. Rushton*)

previously been worn by our grans or mothers. We also had our own theatre, making up our own stories.

Another popular game was marbles, where we dug out shallow holes in the earth and took turns to shoot the marbles in. The marbles we used were made from clay and cost 1*d* for ten. They were called 'marlies'. There were a few coloured-glass marbles, called 'glarneys', but we did not play with these as they were too expensive.

Jacks was a game played with five stones, balanced on the back of the hand, which you threw up in the air, turned your hand over and saw how many you could catch. You could buy official steel jacks, five for 1*d*, but we never bothered with these and collected some steel nuts off the railway track which dropped off the wagons going into the local factories.

We also played hide and seek, of course, and one day there was a story going around that an old, empty house was haunted, so naturally we had to go and investigate. The house stood on its own in a very overgrown garden. The door was swinging open and we crept inside very cautiously. As we approached the stairs, there was a clattering noise and objects began raining down the stairs and we all fled screaming out of the house and never went near the place ever again. However, years later we were telling some of the local lads about this haunted house and they all began laughing and said they had invented the story and waited for us to creep in so they could give us all a great fright by throwing stones down the stairs. So that mystery was cleared up.

One summer when we were sent to bed early before it was dark, we got rather bored so decided to make a telegraph system to send each other messages. We duly collected together all the string we could find and draped it along the back of the houses (built in a continuous row) from one bedroom window to the next. Unfortunately our little scheme was ruined when someone's gran further down the street saw us all at the open back-bedroom windows. We were all ordered back into bed and our string was confiscated.

When I was a bit older, I got a cinematograph for Christmas from my Uncle Sydney, and so the old workshop was duly turned into a cinema (with soapbox seats, of course). My mother gave me all sorts of broken biscuits from the shop and I bought some lemonade crystals for 1*d* and mixed them with cold water for drinks. All the local kids paid 1*d* to see my films. We had a great time and I used to save up all this money in my money box.

When I was about 13, the woman who lived opposite, Mrs Leavesly, thought it would be a good idea if we learned to dance, and she organised a class for the boys and girls in the Conservative Club, teaching us old-time dances like the veleta, St Bernard's Waltz, the military two-step, etc., which were popular at that time. Most of the girls turned up, but only a few lads, who all sat together in one gang and only danced under protest, after the first novelty had worn off.

## Fires

There were several underground fires in the area, where smoke could be seen spiralling up out of the ground, and if you went there at night you could actually see them glow. They were called 'the Fiery Holes' because as the surface seams of coal burnt away the ground collapsed.

We also had quite a few other fires, of course, with some spectacular blazes at local factories, when crowds of people stood on the highest banks to watch. When we were small it was quite exciting to see the fire engine go rushing past with the big brass bell on the front continuously ringing and pulled by two large, black shire horses galloping along.

In 1928, when I was 10 years old, there was a very horrifying incident when my cousin, who was the same age as me, was burnt. No one knew exactly what happened, except that at the time she was alone in her aunty's house with her two small cousins. There was an open fire and somehow she set her clothes on fire. She ran out into the street all on fire and a passer-by jumped off his horse and cart and put out the flames with his coat. She was taken to hospital but was very badly burnt and died shortly afterwards. All the family children went to the funeral; that was the first one that I attended.

## *Winter*

In the winter, when all the pools were frozen over, there were crowds of people skating or sliding about on the ice.

One winter's day – I remember clearly – I was playing with my mice and I heard a really terrifying noise. I went out into the street, along with everyone else, and there was a huge, white airship, called R.101, gliding right overhead. Yes, it really was a sight to remember.

## *Northern Lights*

When I was about 17, during an evening stroll with a friend over some fields between Darlaston and Bilston, just as the light faded, we were surprised to see lovely colours appear in the sky. These gradually got brighter, like an enormous silent firework display, and then faded away. We had no idea what it could be, but next day there was a report in the local paper, the *Express and Star*, reporting a sighting of the Northern Lights, Aurora Borealis, the first time it had been seen in our local area for over 100 years. And every time I see a rainbow in the sky now, it reminds me of the grand show we were very lucky to see so many years ago.

## *Bonfire Night*

Bonfire Night was always a very popular occasion and at that time we all had a holiday from school. We were never allowed to buy our own fireworks, of course, but saved our pocket money for several weeks and waited for Dad to come home from work to take us to get some fireworks. A bonfire was lit in the back yard, potatoes were scrubbed and placed on bricks around the fire, and pots of grey peas were cooked to eat around the fire.

## *Christmas*

Christmas was always an exciting time and I always enjoyed helping to make the Christmas pudding, usually on a cold, dark day in December. We all congregated around the kitchen table and helped in the preparations. My favourite tasks were crumbling the stale bread into crumbs and chopping up the candied peel, which came in half-rounds of peel filled with solidified sugar syrup, which we prised out and ate before chopping up the peel. The large raisins were quite delicious to eat, but all the stones had to be removed before they could be chopped up and put into the pudding. This was a very sticky job and required a handy basin of warm water to remove all the stones from your fingers; it was the least popular job. In addition to the puddings for Christmas and New Year, an extra pudding was made for each birthday during the year.

Christmas trees were not in general fashion either, but instead we had two large, wooden rings covered with cotton wool, tinsel and sweets, etc., which hung from a large hook in the ceiling.

## *Politics*

Elections were usually quite lively occasions for the youngsters and there were processions round the streets, supporting different candidates, singing songs and shouting slogans like 'Down with the dirty yeller' – the colour used by one of the parties. When opposing sides accidentally met, the usual scraps would ensue. It was always a one-sided election in the area, as it was a very safe Labour seat. I never joined in these processions, as my parents supported different political parties. I just listened to all the arguments, where everyone was quite confident their own side was right.

Peace celebrations, Darlaston. These were held at the Town Hall in 1919, following the
end of the First World War. Designed by Jethro Cossins of Birmingham and built by Thomas Tildesley,
the Town Hall also housed a library and was the venue for many recitals and wedding receptions.
(*Mr Ian Bott*)

## The Royal Family

The most popular Royal at this time was without any doubt the Prince
of Wales, a real pin-up person. During the recession in the early 1930s,
he made a tour of the area to cheer everyone up a bit and I remember
walking about three miles from Darlaston to stand for two hours on the
clay banks at Bentley to watch him pass by on his way from Walsall to
Wolverhampton. There were great crowds of people cheering and
waving their Union Jacks. The sun shone all day and we took some
bread and jam and bottles of water to drink, and everyone was happy.

# 7

---

# Carnivals, Fairs
# & the Pictures

Around the 1930s, Darlaston was a thriving, industrial small town and there was always something exciting going on. Every summer there were carnivals in every town and people were kept busy making coloured bunting to hang across the streets. Most people seemed to have a large Union Jack and these were hung out of the bedroom windows. Then there were horses and carts to be decorated with evergreen branches, flowers, etc. for the parade. The larger factories organised jazz bands, mostly girls, in smart uniforms, walking round the town playing popular tunes on 'bazookas' (small wind-blown instrument or whistle).

One year I asked my friend from across the street, Jenny Nicholls, if she would like to enter the carnival parade with me. We decided to become 'the Bisto Kids' and wrote to the firm for some advice; they sent us some advertising posters and a couple of 'Bisto Kids' costumes, which we had to adjust as they were much too big. We begged a couple of old caps and two pairs of very old boots, which we made to match the Bisto adverts by making a gaping hole in the toes. My dad made us a copy of the wooden cart, also from an advert picture, and we stuck Bisto posters all over it and joined the crowds of other entrants for the official judging

Edie's brother, Wilfred Whitehouse, posing in carnival costume. (*Mrs E. Rushton*)

**Darlaston Hospitals Carnival,**
1931.

**Certificate of Merit**

This is to Certify that *Edith Whitehouse*
appeared in the above Carnival as *Bisto Kids*
and was awarded *First Prize*

*J. J. Hunt* Chairman.

*J. W. Kirk* Secretary.

July 19th, 1931.

Chris. Wilkes, Darlaston Printing Works, King Street (Phone 257)

The certificate won by Edie and her friend Jenny Nicholls for winning first prize for their entry as 'the Bisto Kids' in the Darlaston Hospitals Carnival, 1931. (*Mrs E. Rushton*)

before the parade began. We were very excited to win first prize, which was 15*s*. It was presented to us at a dance in the Town Hall in the evening, and we had 7*s* 6*d* each and posted the costumes back to Bisto, as requested.

## The Wakes Week

We all looked forward to the Wakes Week, when Pat Collins' Fair arrived, every year in August. It was held at the bottom of Pinfold Street in Darlaston, in a place kept specially for the Wake. All the family used to go; it was a special occasion. You could have a ride on the big horses for 1*d* and listen to the organ music. That was always my favourite, because I always liked horses. The fair had big swingboats, which held about twelve people. There was a cakewalk, which was a large platform that kept moving from side to side as you tried to walk along it; that was fun and we all liked that. Everything cost 1*d* or 2*d* on Saturday night.

There were lots of games, like throwing balls in buckets, which we always had a go at because if you knew the way to throw the ball in the bucket, you won every time. The idea is you never throw the ball into the bucket in front of you because it hits the bottom of the bucket and bounces straight out again, but if you aim to one side, the ball hits the side, goes round and round the side of the bucket and then just falls to the

Darlaston Wakes, 25 August 1948. (*Mr Ned Williams*)

A Pat Collins Fair, 1930s. (*Mr Ned Williams*)

bottom, and then you get your prize, usually a coconut. Most of the prizes were coconuts and they never seemed to run out of them, so we all looked forward to Wakes Week and getting a coconut. You never saw them any other time. There were also shooting galleries with targets and you could win a goldfish in a bowl. I wasn't old enough to shoot; you had to be grown up – about 14. My dad never had a go on the shooting stand.

Every August when the fair arrived, we used to make our own games stalls along the street outside our houses, which were copies of the originals but made out of old cardboard boxes. No money was used, just old buttons; the bigger the button, the more goes you had, so buttons used to mysteriously disappear from clothes quite often during Wakes Week.

## The Pictures

Most Saturday afternoons we went to the pictures, usually the Olympia, to watch black and white silent films, where a lady always sat at the front, playing the piano with appropriate music. We paid 2*d* in the back seats and 1*d* at the front. There was always a long queue waiting for the doors to open, and most weeks a few fights took place, some of which carried on inside, too. Opposite the entrance, there was a small shop selling sweets and home-made pop. The pop was very popular, and if

The Olympia Cinema, Darlaston. Its main entrance was in Blockall. (*Walsall Local History Society*)

75

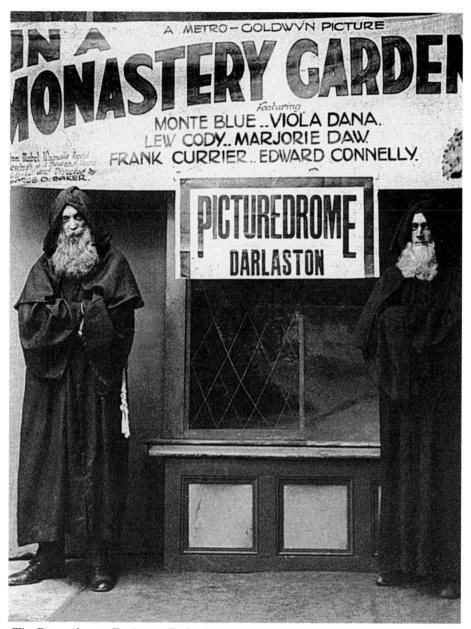

The Picturedrome, Darlaston. Before he commenced in business as a cycle dealer, Len Mitchell was a pianist for the silent movies and was also the piano tuner for schools in the Darlaston district. Here, he is pictured standing to the left of the pay booth at the Picturedrome, Crescent Road in 1925, while promoting the film *In a Monastery Garden*. (*Mrs Marion Evans*)

you were a bit late it was all sold out. It was only 1*d* a bottle and you got ½*d* back when you returned the bottle. Occasionally we went to the Picturedrome, but that was more expensive.

Some years later the 'talkies' arrived, with Al Jonson singing, and the piano lady disappeared. Eventually the old cinema was closed down. It was declared unsafe because the ground underneath it was on fire and caused the foundations to collapse.

# 8

## School Days

School days began at 5 years old and our nearest infant school was in Salisbury Street, about twenty minutes' walk, so groups of local children were accompanied to school by one of the parents. All the teachers were women, but children were mostly very well behaved in school and sat in rows of wooden desks. One boy, called Freddy, was not so well behaved, and one day he threw the inkpot at the teacher and got caned. The best students sat in the back rows of the class, and the ones needing extra attention sat in the front rows for the teacher to keep an eye on them.

At school we just did reading, writing and arithmetic and had to learn our tables. Writing was printing in capital letters and figures and, later, practising joined-up letters. We did a lot of copying from the blackboard and reading from textbooks – storybooks. I quite enjoyed school and never had any problems.

When we got to about 10 years old, the boys played football in the playground for one lesson, while the girls had to do needlework. I never thought this was fair as I found sewing boring, so kept looking through the window, wishing I was outside playing football. Needless to say, my needlework never got finished. I was still working on the same bit at the end of the year because I had to keep taking out the stitches and redoing them as my efforts weren't good enough. From 11 to 14 years, boys and girls attended separate secondary schools and I went to Dorsett Road School.

There were no school dinners or milk, so if you could not get home you just had a sandwich. Later, when Horlicks malted milk arrived and you could afford 1$d$ a day, you could get a nice cup of hot Horlicks at break time, made by the headmistress in a large urn in which she boiled the water. (I still enjoy my cup of Horlicks today.) During the two-hour lunch break, some children had to run home and collect their dad's dinner, already cooked at home, and take it to the factory where he worked. It was usually hot stew in a basin, which had to be delivered as quickly as possible before it got cold.

One Christmas I was given a present by the teacher, as I was top of the class. It was a chocolate Father Christmas and I proudly took it home and put it on display on the sideboard. So when my brother arrived and picked it up, bit off the head and ate it, I was quite upset.

When I was about 10, the headmistress wanted to enter me for an exam to go to Bilston Girls' High School, as I was the only one in the school who she thought might pass; but I never took the exam. I was not at all keen on the idea and preferred to stay with all my friends. Around this time, we had been reading *Gulliver's Travels* at school and I began having nightmares. Every night I had the same dream that I was being tied down with ropes by hundreds of little men so I couldn't walk, and once I got up and walked in my sleep and went downstairs, where I was followed by my dad, who found me under the table searching among the shoes. When he told me it was time to go back to bed, I told him that I couldn't find my skipping rope, but he took me back to bed and I went off to sleep. The doctor said it was probably because of my age and I might be a bit anaemic, so he gave me some Iron Jelloids. But my mother thought it might be connected with the extra work for the exam and decided not to let me take it, so I went happily with all my friends to the secondary school. However, my teacher wasn't very pleased as she was keen to have a success and I was her best hope.

Edie in her early teenage years in the back yard at 39 Foster Street, Darlaston.
(*Mrs E. Rushton*)

At about that time, whenever I went to get my hair cut, I used to pass out. The barber would laugh when I walked in and sat down, and he would say, 'Don't faint today. We've run out of brandy.' Strange to say, I've never been very keen on hairdressers since.

When I got to the secondary school, the girls were allowed to play some games, such as dodgeball. In this, everyone stood round in a ring, with one in the middle who had a rather large ball rolled at their legs, which they had to try and avoid. If they were hit, someone else went in the middle. We also played netball and rounders. When I was about 12, they opened up a cookery course, which I rather liked. Also, my brother liked the things I made and brought home from school, and soon ate them all up.

# 9

## Starting Work

When I was coming up to 14 years old and would soon have to leave school, I became interested in secretarial work. My Uncle Sydney said I could have some shorthand and typing lessons and he arranged for me to take some private lessons with a local teacher one evening a week, which I quite enjoyed. My mother paid for the lessons − 1s 6d per week. When I left school at the age of 14, there was a period of deep depression and very little work available and I spent hours in long queues waiting for interviews in Darlaston, Wednesbury, Willenhall, Bilston and even Birmingham − no luck anywhere. But I was then able to enrol for a free commercial course at the local college when the autumn term began, and I went there five nights a week, doing more typing, shorthand, English, maths and book-keeping. At the end of each term I passed in all the subjects and thereby got a free entry to the following term.

I still had no job, however, and after a few months my mother said I couldn't stay at home any longer doing nothing and I would have to go into the local bolt and nut factory, where a few jobs were available. So I duly began working at the Steel Nut and Joseph Hampton Factory in Wednesbury. It was the most miserable and unhappy period of my whole life. We worked from 7.30 in the morning until 6.00 in the evening, five days a week. It was dirty, smelly, noisy and totally

Going on a date? Edie in the back yard of the Foster Street house, wearing a pretty, lacy dress, *c.* 1935. (*Mrs E. Rushton*)

exhausting. We had to clean out the swarf from underneath long lines of very noisy automatic bolt and nut machines and drag it away in heavy steel boxes. It really was slave labour – the wages 6s (30p) per week.

After about six months I managed to get a job in the warehouse, helping to weigh out and pack bolts and nuts, which was a little better and not so noisy. Then a vacancy arose in the office typing pool and Uncle Syd managed to get me in there as a junior typist. The wages were about the same but it was like heaven after the factory. I spent seven years, altogether, attending evening classes, getting certificates – UEI or RSA, or touchtyping and shorthand at 60, 80, 100 and 120 words per minute – and I had just begun a teachers' training course for Pitman's Shorthand when the war broke out and I had to give it up.

## Outings with Workmates

I joined the Works Sports Club and began playing tennis, and there were Saturday night dances in the works canteen, which I quite enjoyed. I went out for bike rides with some of the lads in the office on my brand-new bike, thanks to my dear gran and the little leather bag of golden sovereigns she had saved up from the shop and left me. I really loved my bike. It was like another world of freedom and I used it all the time – cleaned and polished it every week. At weekends I went to lots of local beauty spots. I went to work on it every single day and when I came home I had my tea and went back on my bike for the evening classes at Wednesbury Commercial College.

A few months after I began working in the office, another young girl, named Marjorie, joined our team. There were eight of us sitting around a large table, all under the control of an older lady, Miss Fletcher. Marjorie had the same surname as me – Whitehouse – but was not related. She was about a year older and lived in Wednesbury and we

Always happy to pose! Edie in the back yard at No. 39, *c.* 1935. (*Mrs E. Rushton*)

became friends. One day she asked me if I would go with her to a Saturday night dance in Wednesbury Town Hall. She said her twin brother would give me a lift back to Darlaston after the dance, as I couldn't really ride my bike in a long dance dress. I travelled there on the tram and met my friend Marjorie and another girl from Wednesbury. Ray, the twin brother, did not come to the dance but Marjorie said not to worry – he would definitely come to take all three of us back home after the dance and he was going to drop me off first and then return to the Town Hall to pick up the other two.

We enjoyed the dance and Ray arrived promptly to collect me but when I saw the car I couldn't believe my eyes. It was quite enormous. It was in fact the Mayor's car, which he had borrowed because his dad was Mayor of Wednesbury at the time, and I really felt honoured to be getting a lift home in the Mayor's car. On the way home it was getting a bit misty, but no problem, and I was dropped off right outside my door in about ten minutes. I said thanks very much, and he turned the car around and set off back to Wednesbury to collect his sister and her friend.

The following Monday morning I was very surprised to receive an irate telephone call from Majorie's friend, accusing me of delaying Ray while they were waiting outside the Town Hall to be picked up and taken home. It seems they had waited for about half an hour in the freezing cold and then decided to walk home. On the Monday morning, Marjorie had not turned up for work and there was a phone call to say she had to stay in bed with a very bad cold. This was all very puzzling to me but I found out later that Ray had run into some dense fog on the way back to Wednesbury and had an accident with a large slow-moving lorry carrying a load of steel tubes overhanging the back, poorly lit and with just a small piece of white material tied on at the back. Ray had collided with the back end of the load and all the steel tubes had gone through the windscreen, making quite a mess of the Mayor's car. Fortunately Ray escaped injury and I heard no more about that.

# 10

Family Cars
& Holidays

Our first car was a blue four-door Standard 8 saloon (registration number DRF 320) and was a shared car which we bought in 1938. It was twelve months old and cost £65. Mom and Dad paid £25 each, I paid £10 and my brother only £5, as he was not quite old enough to drive. I was then 20 years old and the first in the family to learn to drive. I went out for a couple of hours three times a week with a family friend who was a lorry driver. After six weeks I passed my driving test and was then able to accompany my dad in the car until he passed his test. Later on I was also allowed to do the same for my boyfriend, who didn't have a car of his own. My brother Wilfred was upset because he wasn't old enough to get a licence, but he soon caught up with us a few years later.

Shortly after I passed my driving test, the Tower Cinema at West Bromwich began a series of films starting at midnight called 'Saturday midnight matinees'. I managed to persuade my parents to let me take the family car and went with my boyfriend to the first performance. When we came out there was a slight panic because the car had a flat tyre. We had no tools and no idea what to do but some kind people in the car park helped us out and I was able to drive back home to

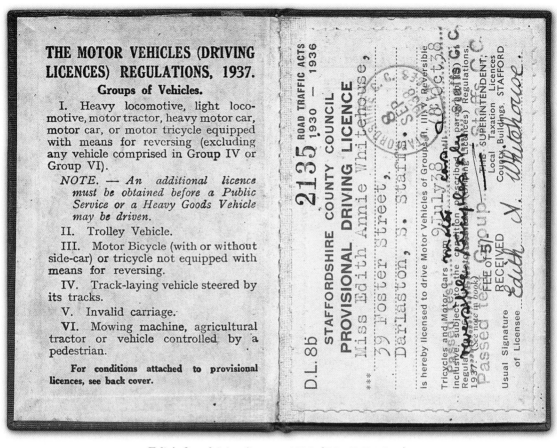

**THE MOTOR VEHICLES (DRIVING LICENCES) REGULATIONS, 1937.**

**Groups of Vehicles.**

I. Heavy locomotive, light locomotive, motor tractor, heavy motor car, motor car, or motor tricycle equipped with means for reversing (excluding any vehicle comprised in Group IV or Group VI).

*NOTE. — An additional licence must be obtained before a Public Service or a Heavy Goods Vehicle may be driven.*

II. Trolley Vehicle.

III. Motor Bicycle (with or without side-car) or tricycle not equipped with means for reversing.

IV. Track-laying vehicle steered by its tracks.

V. Invalid carriage.

VI. Mowing machine, agricultural tractor or vehicle controlled by a pedestrian.

**For conditions attached to provisional licences, see back cover.**

D.L.8b

ROAD TRAFFIC ACTS 1930 — 1936

2135

STAFFORDSHIRE COUNTY COUNCIL

PROVISIONAL DRIVING LICENCE

Miss Edith Annie Whitehouse, 39 Foster Street, Darlaston, S. Staffs.

Is hereby licensed to drive Motor Vehicles of Groups I, III, V

Tricycles and Motor Cars

THE SUPERINTENDENT, Local Taxation Licences County Buildings, STAFFORD

Usual Signature of Licensee *Edith A. Whitehouse.*

Edie's first driving licence, 1938. (*Mrs E. Rushton*)

Darlaston. We kept this car for about a year and then exchanged it for a maroon Flying Standard 10 (BFD 915). This was followed by a Ford 8 (EMY 360), which we called 'Emmie'.

When I was young, there were no paid holidays so not many people went away for a holiday. We just had day trips on bank holidays to Blackpool, Rhyl, Kinver, etc., travelling by train from James Bridge station in Darlaston. The first time I went away for a week's holiday, I was 15 and my friend, Dorothy Purslow, invited me to join her and her mom and dad

Exterior of wholesale Sunday newsagents W.F. Taylor & Sons in High Street, Darlaston, *c.* 1939. John L. Taylor is on the left of the picture with his friend Tom Lawley. The house to the right of the shop eventually became Hale's betting shop. The Taylors' Standard 10 car outside the shop is the same model as that owned by Edie's family.

(*Mr Bill Taylor*)

Sunday newspaper roundsmen prior to boarding one of Davenport's Luxury Coaches for their day trip, organised by Mr William Taylor, proprietor of W.F. Taylor & Sons, wholesale Sunday newsagents, *c.* 1937. W.H. Smith, a large newsagent, frowned on Sunday working, which enabled smaller concerns to benefit. The roundsmen had no shops, but collected the papers from Taylors and carried them in a trolley or newspaper bag to sell door-to-door. From left to right, front row: Bill Taylor (son of William Taylor), Joe Laban, next to his father, also Joe Laban, Mr Powers (Joe's father-in-law), two young Knight boys. In the back row, on the extreme right, is Mr William Taylor; fourth from the right (hatless) is Mr Sam Russell, who later opened his own shop on the Walsall Road, Darlaston. (*Mr Bill Taylor*)

for a week in Blackpool, and this was really great. While we were there I had my first trip in an aeroplane when me and my friend had a trip from Squires Gate Airport out over the sea and around Blackpool Tower in a two-seater biplane. It was very, very noisy but we both enjoyed it and it cost us 5s each, which was a lot of money then.

Edie and friend Dorothy Purslow enjoying a donkey ride on Blackpool beach in July 1934. (*Mrs E. Rushton*)

The aeroplane in which Edie and friend Dorothy Purslow had their first, exciting trip round Blackpool in 1934. (*Mrs E. Rushton*)

Edie's father, Joseph Whitehouse, and family friend Bertie Johnson (with dog) on a day out at Blackpool in May 1934. (*Mrs E. Rushton*)

Edie's parents, Joseph and Winifred Whitehouse, enjoying a ride in a paddleboat. (*Mrs E. Rushton*)

Edie's father, Joseph Whitehouse, paddling in the sea at Blackpool. Note the smart jacket, collar and tie! (*Mrs E. Rushton*)

The Whitehouse family and friends on the beach at Blackpool. From left to right, back row: Mr Salt, Wilfred and Winifred Whitehouse; front row: Mrs Salt, Edie, Joseph Whitehouse and Bertie Johnson.
(*Mrs E. Rushton*)

From left to right: Wilfred, Winifred and Edie Whitehouse sitting on Blackpool beach in 1933.
(*Mrs E. Rushton*)

Edie and Wilfred Whitehouse in bathing costumes, paddling in the sea at Colwyn Bay, *c.* 1933. (*Mrs E. Rushton*)

From left to right: Edie, Joseph and Winifred Whitehouse sitting on Blackpool beach in 1933. (*Mrs E. Rushton*)

Posing for the parents! Edie (aged 6) with brother Wilfred (aged 2), mounted on a wooden horse in Charles Howell's Studios, Blackpool. (*Mrs E. Rushton*)

When I was 18, I was allowed to go for a week's holiday at the South Devon Holiday Camp in Paignton with my boyfriend, Wilf. It was great: tennis courts, swimming pool, coach trips and nice, sunny weather. We were really enjoying ourselves until, unfortunately, halfway through the week, a painful swelling developed under my armpit. I had to go to see a doctor, who lanced the abscess for me. I didn't allow this to ruin my week but there was no more tennis or swimming for the remainder of the holiday.

Happy days. Edie with boyfriend Wilfred Rushton sitting on the diving board at South Devon Holiday Camp in 1936. (*Mrs E. Rushton*)

Fun in the pool at South Devon Holiday Camp, 1936. (*Mrs E. Rushton*)

Enjoying a pint at South Devon Holiday Camp, 1936. Edie is in the front row, with Wilf at the extreme right of the back row. (*Mrs E. Rushton*)

# 11

## Wartime

When war was declared with Germany in 1939, lots of men were called up for active service, but if you worked in a factory making equipment for war use, you were exempted. All scrap iron was collected and lots of iron railings were removed and melted down to be made into nuts and bolts, etc. for use in the war effort.

Rationing of food, clothes and petrol was introduced and only doctors were allowed to buy non-rationed petrol. Coupons were issued for buying bread, butter, bacon, meat and jars of jam, etc., but fruit and vegetables were not rationed and all the allotments were well used. Items like bananas and oranges were quite rare and if any shop got a delivery, word spread around very quickly and a long queue soon appeared, so the whole delivery was quickly sold.

Our family was quite lucky with Mom's little shop as we always had lots of extra food from the stocks of tinned food in the storeroom – corned beef, salmon, crab, pilchards, sardines, peas and baked beans, etc. – which was not included in the rationing. In fact, the only item we really missed was sugar and my mom quickly decided to drink her tea with no sugar, so the rest of us got a bit extra. Before very long, a black market grew up in the sale of coupons, mainly for clothes and petrol.

Petrol coupons issued by the Ministry of Fuel and Power during the Second World War. (*Mrs E. Rushton*)

Air-raid shelters were built in back yards and when bomber planes were approaching, the air-raid signals sounded and people went into the shelters until the 'all clear' went. Some factories had to close for a time, and workers moved out and collected mainly in the car parks. Most of the air raids came during the night when we were in bed. We didn't go

Wardens from 'C' group of Darlaston
Civil Defence contingent, June 1943.
(*Mr Jack Aston*)

The cadets of Darlaston Air Training Corps at Newton air base, Nottinghamshire, 1945.
(*Mr Horace Page*)

outside to the air-raid shelters but got out of bed, took a blanket and pillow and went down into the coal cellar to wait for the 'all clear' before we could return to the luxury of a nice, warm bed.

Coventry and Birmingham were worst hit in the air raids. Where we lived, in Darlaston, it was quite industrialised, with factories among houses in most streets. Richards' Bolt and Nut factory was opposite to where we lived and there were at least five other factories close by, but although a few odd bombs fell in the area, not a single one found a factory and no one was killed or injured. One bomb did make a direct hit on All Saints Church, which was completely demolished, but rebuilt after the war. After a while, we were all issued with gas masks, and babies were given special gas bags in which they were completely enclosed.

In the early 1940s, as there was no petrol for private cars due to the war, we decided one fine Sunday morning to have an outing by bus to Kingswood Common. The bus from Wolverhampton was packed, mainly with armed forces personnel, standing in the aisles. I did manage to get a seat and an air force chappie stuffed his very heavy kitbag on the rack above me and as the bus turned a sharp corner, it came crashing down on top of my head. The bus driver immediately stopped the bus and came to ask if I was OK. I certainly felt quite shaken and a bit woozy, but no serious damage, although the weight of the bag had banged my teeth together very hard and chipped two of my front teeth. When I mentioned this to the bus driver he said, 'Are they false teeth, Madam?' I said, 'No.' I was only just turned 20 at the time. At that, the bus driver then said, 'Oh, that's a pity. If they'd been false teeth you could have put in a claim for some new ones.' I completely dismissed this unfortunate incident from my mind but, a few years later, my front teeth began to disintegrate and had to be taken out; looking back, I believe it was all a result of the crash. So although I had my first dental plate in my early twenties, fortunately it was free, as the National Health Service had just come into operation in 1948, two years after the war ended.

# 12

---

# Love & Marriage

It was through my bike that I first met my future husband, Wilf, when I was 15. One May Bank Holiday, I went for a bike ride with my friend Amelia Price to Barr Beacon, where we spent the afternoon with a couple of lads from West Bromwich, also out for a ride. That summer I went out for lots of nice rides with Wilf, but unfortunately we never got very far because he had a very old bike which his older brother had bought cheap and had repaired for him. The repairs didn't stretch to new tyres so he kept getting punctures and walking back to West Bromwich, pushing his old bike. At the end of the summer we lost touch with each other for about three years, until we met again by accident as he was pushing his bike past the Commercial College in Wednesbury. We resumed our friendship and bike rides, as by this time he had left school, was working, and could afford a better bike (he was then 17 and I was 18).

When war broke out, Wilf was working in the booking office at West Bromwich, Great Western Railway station. He decided to volunteer to join the RAF but, as he was working in transport, he was automatically drafted into the army in the Royal Engineers, which he didn't like at all as he found himself doing route marches, square bashing and digging trenches. Fortunately for Wilf, radar (all very secretive) was then invented and he was selected to go on a special course at Malvern

An early photo of Edie's future husband, Wilfred Rushton (right of picture),
and his friend Bill Scott on an outing with bikes to Barr Beacon in May 1934.
(*Mrs E. Rushton*)

College. There he learned how to maintain and repair the radar sets
being used by the ack-ack units to locate and destroy approaching enemy
aircraft and, later on, the flying bombs causing a lot of devastation round
London. He spent most of the wartime years in and around London,

Edie's future husband, Wilfred Rushton, at Barr Beacon in 1937. (*Mrs E. Rushton*)

Edie relaxing in Sutton Park after cycling there in August 1934. (*Mrs E. Rushton*)

Young sweethearts. Edie with Wilf Rushton on a day out to Bewdley, July 1936.
(*Mrs E. Rushton*)

often working 48 hours at a stretch with no sleep. He was promoted to lance corporal, then corporal, sergeant and, finally, staff sergeant.

We missed each other very much, so decided to get married when he came home on leave. I saved up all my clothing coupons and bought a lovely wedding dress. Wilf only just made it to the church on time as my

dad's car broke down when my brother went to pick him up from the station. Between them they managed to get the car going again, but Wilf had to get married with hands covered in black grease as there was no time to wash before the service. We had a very happy wedding day, followed by a party for family and friends.

Edie and Wilfred Rushton's group wedding photo, 28 September 1940. From left to right: Barbara Rushton (Wilf's niece); Barbara's mother, Olive Rushton; Selina Rushton (Wilf's mother); Arthur Rushton (Wilf's older brother); Wilf and Edie; Jacqueline Bliss (Edie's bridesmaid); Winifred Whitehouse (Edie's mother); Sydney Whitehouse (Edie's uncle), Joseph Whitehouse (Edie's father); Eileen Johnson (daughter of family friends Eva and Bertie Johnson). (*Mrs E. Rushton*)

The happy couple. Edie's wedding to Wilfred Rushton (Lance Corporal, Royal Engineers) at St Lawrence's Church, Darlaston on 28 September 1940. (*Mrs E. Rushton*)

Edie with her bridesmaid, Jacqueline Bliss, on 28 September 1940.
(*Mrs E. Rushton*)

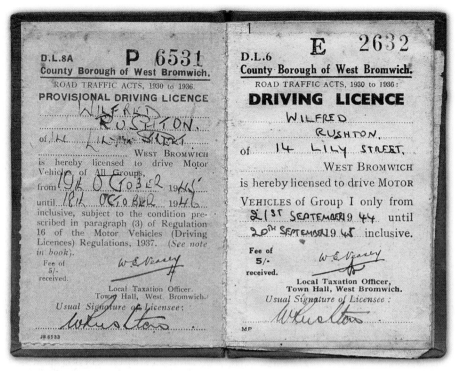

*Above:* The first driving licence for Edie's husband, Wilfred Rushton. (*Mrs E. Rushton*)
*Below, left*: An army paybook belonging to Wilfred Rushton. (*Mrs E. Rushton*)

Towards the end of the war, Wilf was posted to Trieste in northern Italy. He was offered a commission as captain, but did not accept; he had no wish to make a career of army life and just wanted to return home as soon as possible, as we had a lovely baby girl named Patricia. When the war ended, Wilf was finally demobbed in 1946, and came home with a nice tan from time spent on the beaches in Italy. Patricia now had a baby sister named Jean, and we all went for a week's holiday in Barmouth to celebrate Wilf's homecoming before he returned to work.

An Aston Studio portrait, taken in 1945, shows Edie with daughters Patricia and Jean
(who obviously didn't like the photographer!). (*Mrs E. Rushton*)

Film star material? Edie as a young woman, wearing an
embroidered blouse. (*Mrs E. Rushton*)

# Acknowledgements

The author expresses her thanks to the following for their help and support, and in particular for the loan of their photographs included in this book:

Mrs Patricia Oakley, Mr Brian Whitehouse, Mr David Cairns, Mrs Jean Cairns, Dr Carl Chinn, Mr Ian Bott, Mr Terry Price, Mrs Marion Evans, Mr Jack Aston, Mr Horace Page, Mr Bill Taylor, Mr Howard Madeley, Mr John Sutton, Mr Stan Griffiths, Mr Terry Smitheman, Mr Ned Williams, Darlaston Local History Society, Walsall Local History Society.

# THE BLACK COUNTRY SOCIETY

The Black Country Society is proud to be associated with **Sutton Publishing** of Stroud. In 1994 the society was invited by Sutton Publishing to collaborate in what has proved to be a highly successful publishing partnership, namely the extension of the **Britain in Old Photographs** series into the Black Country. In this joint venture the Black Country Society has played an important role in establishing and developing a major contribution to the region's photographic archives by encouraging society members to compile books of photographs of the area or town in which they live.

The first book in the Black Country series was *Wednesbury in Old Photographs* by Ian Bott, launched by Lord Archer of Sandwell in November 1994. Since then almost 70 Black Country titles have been published. The total number of photographs contained in these books is in excess of 13,000, suggesting that the whole collection is probably the largest regional photographic survey of its type in any part of the country to date.

This voluntary society was founded in 1967 as a reaction to the trends of the late 1950s and early '60s. This was a time when the reorganisation of local government was seen as a threat to the identity of individual communities and when, in the name of progress and modernisation, the industrial heritage of the Black Country was in danger of being swept away.

The general aims of the society are to stimulate interest in the past, present and future of the Black Country, and to secure at regional and national levels an accurate understanding and portrayal of what constitutes the Black Country and, wherever possible, to encourage and facilitate the preservation of the Black Country's heritage.

The society, which now has over 2,500 members worldwide, organises a yearly programme of activities. There are six venues in the Black Country where evening meetings are held on a monthly basis from September to April. In the summer months, there are fortnightly guided evening walks in the Black Country and its green borderland, and there is also a full programme of excursions further afield by car. Details of all these activities are to be found on the society's website, **www.blackcountrysociety.co.uk**, and in *The Blackcountryman*, the quarterly magazine that is distributed to all members.

*PO Box 71 · Kingswinford · West Midlands DY6 9YN*